creat!ve confirmation

# Parent Conversations

by Ralph W. Yernberg

Augsburg Fortress, Minneapolis

# Contents ◆
## Parent Conversations




**Creative Confirmation Series**
*Parent Conversations*

Editors: Randi Sundet Griner, Eileen K. Zahn, and Julie A. Lindesmith
Designer: Connie Helgeson-Moen

Cover Photographers: Jeff Greenberg/Unicorn Stock Photos (front); © CLEO Freelance Photo (back)

Scripture Acknowledgment: Unless otherwise marked, scripture quotations are from New Revised Standard Version Bible, copyright 1989 Division of Christian Education of the National Council of the Churches of Christ in the United States of America. Used by permission.





Manufactured in U.S.A.
1 2 3 4 5 6 7 8 9 0 1 2 3 4 5 6 7 8 9

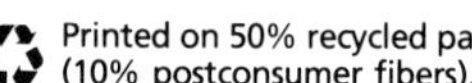
Printed on 50% recycled paper (10% postconsumer fibers).

# Introduction

## CREATIVE CONFIRMATION

Welcome to the Creative Confirmation Series. This series invites you to customize a confirmation program that meets the needs of your youth and your congregation. These flexible confirmation resources work together through active and experiential learning activities to emphasize basic Bible literacy, the Small Catechism, worship, and daily life in the Christian community.

**LEADER RESOURCES** Nine resource books are provided for pastors and leaders. *Bible 1, Bible 2, Bible 3,* and *Small Catechism* serve as the core of the program. The other five leader resources—*Worship, Community-Building Activities and Games, Sharing the Language of Faith, Mission/Service Projects*, and *Parent Conversations*—help you build a comprehensive confirmation program by providing related activities that nurture faith development in a community setting. The sessions are designed for a group of up to 12 middle school students.

**LEARNER RESOURCES** *Study Bible: The New Student Bible NRSV* (Augsburg Fortress code 30-10-999) and *A Contemporary Translation of Luther's Small Catechism: Study Edition* (Augsburg Fortress code 15 5305) are the primary student resources for Creative Confirmation sessions. In some sessions a reproducible page from the leader resource is used. The *Youth Journal* guides learner reflection on many of the sessions in *Bible 1, Bible 2, Bible 3, Small Catechism, Worship,* and *Sharing the Language of Faith.* In session plans, look for the ✎ symbol and page number that point to a *Youth Journal* activity.

**About *Parent Conversations*** ◆ *Parent Conversations* is one of the leader resources for Creative Confirmation. The first part of this resource provides ideas and discussion formats that encourage dialogue between parents/guardians and youth. The second part provides ideas and formats that encourage discussions among groups of parents. This resource will help youth and their leaders:

◆ discuss experiences and topics of interest;
◆ share personal faith stories and build supportive relationships;
◆ develop relationships that encourage personal growth for the strengthening of families and the community of faith.

**USING THIS RESOURCE** The 19 parent-youth boundary breaker sessions in this book each last about 10 minutes, and could take place regularly during the last portion of classtime throughout the year. Or, it may work well in your congregation to plan two or three special meeting times through the year where several of the boundary breakers could be discussed, perhaps over a simple meal.

In addition, the 24 parent-to-parent conversations included could take place during the time youth are in class, or at another time that works for parents in your setting.

This resource will help youth and their leaders share personal faith stories and build supportive relationships.

# Parent-Youth Interchanges

Youth are different today from 20 years ago. The same might be said about the parents or the adults who care about them. Youth are different because there are different challenges in their culture. They have had to respond to these challenges in new ways. Often the journey they walk, they walk alone—without the benefit of caring adults to guide and support them.

What makes their culture different? Each generation can lay claim to specific stresses that challenge the young. The youth of the last century may have skipped the in-between years—what we call adolescence—entirely. They were children until they were old or strong enough to work. Then they became adults.

Today adolescence itself is being challenged. Once thought to be those years of dramatic growth, when a self-identity was built, adolescence now begins earlier and ends later. Because of economic realities, young people can leave their teenage years with enormous debt from college loans, and degrees that do not help them find jobs. The result can be an extended dependence economically and emotionally on parents or guardians who once believed these same people would be on their own.

In between, there are the new stresses of an increase in awareness of violence, guns in the schoolroom, rampant drug abuse, sophisticated diseases that spread through sexual contact, and the constant push to succeed in sports and leadership by well-meaning parents.

How does the church respond to the pressures of raising children in a culture filled with images that distort life? How can church leaders assist an honest interchange between young people and the adults who care for them? How does the adult world learn to enter into the culture of the young in order to support, affirm, and challenge with positive messages of hope?

That is the topic of this resource book. Clearly, it is an important topic for parents and guardians, church leaders, and for any adult who cares about a young person. We are engaged in a battle for the imagination of our young people. The images that are part of youth culture, the sounds that explode through their headphones, all seek to drown out messages of truth that the church seeks to proclaim through the gospel. They may not be in head-to-head combat. It is more challenging than that! It is simply that too often the good news of Jesus Christ is not presented in an engaging and imaginative way.

The confirmation process is a program not only for confirmands, for young adolescents. It is a process that applies to their parents or guardians as well. As a church, we need to find ways to communicate with the young people entrusted to our care. As a church, we need to find ways to communicate to parents, sponsors, and caring adults so that they too might hear the message of Christian growth. Together we seek an interchange of ideas that will foster creative hope in the new creation that is the promise of Jesus Christ.

What do we know about our confirmands? What do we know about their parents or sponsors? Your confirmands are in the midst of the biggest changes in their lives. They are discovering new things about their bodies. They are becoming very sensitive about their weight, shape, and imperfections. Being part of a social sphere is much more important than spending time with family. They are highly energetic and suffer huge swings in their feelings and moods.

In short, they are in the worst possible time of life to be asked to sit down in a church room after a long day at school to learn about God. However, they have serious questions about their faith, are concerned about fairness, about things that go wrong in their relationships, and wish they had better relationships with parents or adults who care about them.

What about the parents or caring adults in their lives? If you ask your confirmands they will most likely complain about their parents' or guardians' lack of flexibility. They will say, "They should lighten up." Most adults who have young adolescents are worried that their children will get into trouble. Many parents fret over whether their children will be successful and want them to be highly involved in school activities.

Other parents, however, are overly tired and find raising children to be an extremely difficult task. Relationships can be filled with guilt as parents fret over lack of quality time. Many homes are not traditional—Mom, Dad, and children. Many children experience divorce and extended family life; some share time between parents. Most parents are unsure about whether their actions are right, whether they did all they could to provide for a positive environment for their young adult.

What do youth and their parents or guardians have in common? They can share a common faith. The research (of James Fowler and others) on the stages of faith is helpful but not at all conclusive. It is, however, safe to suggest that most learners in confirmation are at an early stage of their faith development. We might call it a "naive" stage where their beliefs and values are based upon the language they have heard, and the experiences of the faith community that surrounds them. Rather than an in-depth understanding of a triune God, they will have a basic view that "God is love" or "Jesus is God." The faith of a confirmand, though growing, is still young. They are on a journey where there is the possibility of momentous discovery and growth.

If the common ground is faith, where are parents and guardians in terms of *their* faith? Many parents and guardians claim that they are at the same place as described above! Unless the parent or guardian has been deeply involved in their own Christian faith journey, they might have a "naive faith" as well. Without opportunity for discussion and study, without involvement in church worship life, a parent might not feel capable of offering much spiritual instruction.

Some of the most avid supporters of traditional confirmation programs are those who are not active in church and seek a quasi-graduation from confirmation for their children. Other parents or guardians are at differing stages of faith. Some may understand their faith as integrally connected with their lives, seeing their vocation as an opportunity to serve God.

The questions and activities that follow seek to enable youth and adults to meet on the common ground of faith. It will be important to avoid value judgments about what some may consider a "correct" understanding of faith. Faith is a journey where content is gathered along the way. What we seek in these discussions is conversation enabling young people to find support and affirmation of the principles guiding their new awareness of God's power in their lives. At the same time, adults are encouraged to know that their understanding of God has meaning for their children. Together, through discussion and action, both can grow in the conviction that the gospel empowers them to love and serve to the glory of God.

Too often the good news of Jesus Christ is not presented in an engaging and imaginative way.

## Parent-youth boundary breakers

# Introduction

The boundary breaker questions that follow seek to provide adults and youth a chance to communicate. To break the boundaries that separate the young and the old, encourage the participants to agree to a covenant that will promote openness to ideas in a nonthreatening manner. Ask each group to list possible covenant agreements such as:

- Listen until the speaker is finished.
- Avoid the use of the phrase "I disagree."
- Rephrase the words of the person to whom you are listening, to ensure understanding.
- Remain in direct eye contact with each other.

For the discussions, arrange various kinds of small groups as appropriate to your needs. These might take place during the last 15 minutes of class time regularly, or several times a year. Several of these topics could be discussed over a simple meal together at the church. Conversations can take place in parent/youth teams, or in groups of four to six youth and adults. Parents need not always be in the same group as their child. Take approximately 10 minutes for each series of questions. You may wish to encourage follow-up discussions that can be done later in the home.

## Boundary breaker 1

# Things I enjoy

A community of friends is marked by signs of friendship. Some of these signs include laughter, support, encouragement, and loyalty. Young and old alike have many interests in their lives to share with each other. These interests can be categorized as "things I enjoy."

Invite the groups to discuss the following:

- Share three things you enjoy doing with others.
- Share three things you enjoy doing alone.
- Describe something you enjoy doing that you do not believe a teenager/adult would enjoy.

## Boundary breaker 2

# My surroundings

Our surroundings often affect what we do and with whom we do it. If there are many children in a family, our rooms may not be private. Some of our surroundings are shared with grandparents or friends. Our surroundings, or our context, can determine how we see life. Our values are, in part, shaped by our surroundings.

Discuss these questions:

- If you could change one thing about where you live, what would it be?
- Finish this statement: "What I like most about where I live is ________."
- If you could move anywhere in the world, where would you go and why?

## Boundary breaker 3

# The world of adults

Sometimes we operate in our own world! A young person may not want to consider the stresses and demands that parents or guardians face. To communicate is to walk in another person's shoes. It is to attempt to be aware of the struggles of another person.

Talk together about these questions. Invite young people to imagine being an adult:

- What do you think adults worry about?
- Do you think adults feel they spend enough time with the people they love the most? Why or why not? (Remember to suspend judgment while listening to answers given here. Strive to learn more about each other.)
- What do you think is the most difficult thing about being a parent/guardian or person charged with raising a teenager today?
- What do you think makes adults happy? Why can they become angry?

## Boundary breaker 4

# Exploring my feelings

A certain smell such as the scent of pine can bring on vivid feelings connected to memories. The scent of a certain spice may remind us of someone we have loved who has passed away. A song may remind us of a person no longer with us whom we miss. A closed-in area may cause us to feel frightened because of a time we were trapped when we were younger.

Explore some of these feelings together:

- Can you think of a time when you were terrified? Have you experienced this feeling recently? What was the cause? *(Note to leader: Questions such as this can create opportunities for a youth who is experiencing some kind of abuse to share about it. If this happens, it is important to discuss with the pastor immediately the appropriate steps that may need to be taken in the interest of the well-being of that youth.)*
- Do certain sounds, smells, or places remind you of events or feelings from the past? Give an example.
- Share a moment when you have felt the happiest.

## Boundary breaker 5

# My future plans

Faith can have a great impact on our plans for the future. Faith can also affect our friendships, volunteer service, our values, and our beliefs. Explore your thoughts about the future with these questions.

- How has your faith been active in what you currently do?
- In what areas might you consider being a volunteer? *(There are many areas of youth volunteer service, including helping in neighborhood sports programs, serving in hospitals, visiting nursing homes, cleaning parks, joining "walks" for good causes, and so forth.)*
- What might parents and youth do together to share faith in their families?

### Boundary breaker 6

# The world of youth

Parents and adults who care for youth are often frightened and concerned about the culture in which youth live and act. The music can seem counterproductive, the dress rebellious, and the situations encountered dangerous. Yet youth are often comfortable in this culture. It is, after all, theirs. And that makes it safe. Being on their own turf implies the need for responsibility. Taking responsibility for their own interests, likes, dislikes, and actions prepares them for future accountability.

Discuss these questions together. Adults may answer them based upon memories of actual experiences during their youth.

- Which activities do (did) you find to be the most enjoyable way to spend your time?
- Name (what) your favorite musical group (was). Why do (did) you like your favorite musical group?
- What is the most difficult problem youth face today (when you were younger)? How do (did) you deal with that problem?

### Boundary breaker 7

# Relationships

Relationships build community. We need others in order for us to be ourselves. We see in others things that we would like to see in ourselves, and sometimes we see things that embarrass us.

In these questions, explore the qualities you would like to find in your relationships:

- What do you think makes for a good relationship with another person?
- What makes for a good relationship with a parent or guardian? What makes for a good relationship with a son or daughter?
- Describe your relationship with God. Describe your relationship with other people. How are they alike?

### Boundary breaker 8

# People who matter

Role models portray positive or negative images to young people. They can play important roles in guiding and influencing the behavior of a person. Rock groups or television characters can influence dress, speech, and behavior. A neighbor, teacher, pastor, or parent can have a profound effect on how a person feels about himself or herself and the identity that subsequently develops.

Use these questions to explore the important people in your lives.

- Name a person who has influenced you and tell how he or she has affected your life.
- Tell about someone to whom you believe you have been important.
- Tell your teenager/parent something positive that you have learned from him or her.

### Boundary breaker 9

# Stresses in my life

Sometimes life seems extremely stressful and uncomfortable. Problems at work, at school, in relationships, or in the community can pose challenging dilemmas. When these stresses occur we can feel depressed, sometimes anxious—in a "fighting mood." Other times we feel hopeless, confused, frustrated. Significant relationships with others and a strong faith can help during these times.

Talk together about these questions:

◆ Describe something stressful for you at this time.

◆ Who helps you work out difficult solutions to hard problems?

◆ How can your faith in God help you deal with the stresses in your life?

### Boundary breaker 10

# Spirit work

The church is called into being through the Spirit as a community in Christ. It is a bridge between the old and the new, between the advent of Jesus and the final day. It is marked with God's grace and love. Yet all too often, the church is criticized for not living up to what it is supposed to be in spirit. People often have strong feelings about their church.

Explore together these questions about your church:

◆ Name five things you like about your congregation.

◆ The church is often called "the body of Christ." Do you feel this name is appropriate to your congregation? Why or why not?

◆ If you could change anything about your congregation, what would it be?

### Boundary breaker 11

# Creation

The Apostles' Creed says we believe that God created all that exists. The world about us can be beautiful. It is also fragile. We care for creation by the ways in which we live—how we use energy, if we use more than our share of resources, and how we care about keeping the earth clean.

Consider together these questions:

◆ Describe one of your favorite places in God's creation. How would you feel if it were destroyed?

◆ How do our actions affect God's creation?

◆ What is the most important environmental issue to you?

◆ Do you believe that you use more than your share of the earth's resources, or do you believe you should have a bigger share? (Resources such as food, material goods, and even our styles of life are based upon using the gifts of creation.)

### Boundary breaker 12

# Faith memories

We often have memories about significant times in our faith journeys. A parent may remember a confirmation service or a funeral and important feelings about the event. A child may remember an important role in a Christmas pageant or a friend's invitation to attend church.

With these questions, explore good memories of important moments in your faith journey:

◆ Share a good memory of something that happened in church.

◆ Who do you think first taught you to pray? If it was a memorized prayer, can you remember it?

◆ Parents: if you were confirmed, share your memory of the event. Youth: how do you think confirmation might help you?

### Boundary breaker 13

# Faith and actions

It is said that faith precedes good works. Our faith has a profound impact on our behavior. We may be motivated to serve God in all we do. On the other hand, service to God through worship and to others through our acts of faith can often be challenging. We may feel pressed for time. We may feel bored.

Explore the relationship between your faith and your actions as you discuss these questions:

◆ How does your faith affect how you treat other people?

◆ Have you ever changed a behavior or thought twice about what you were going to do because it conflicted with your beliefs?

◆ Tell about someone whose faith led her or him into a career or a path of service to others. *(Remember that teachers, homemakers, mechanics, farmers, and others can be ministries of vocation, where service to God and to others is a priority.)*

### Boundary breaker 14

# Childhood memories

Creating good memories fosters strong values in children. Young adults can draw upon their memories as they develop traditions of their own. Memories can also be painful. Some memories need to be forgiven; others need to be healed. Oftentimes, the earliest memories we have can be connected with spirituality.

Talk together about your early childhood memories:

◆ Tell about a good memory you have from when you were very young.

◆ Do you have any memories that are difficult? If you wish, please share one.

◆ Why do you feel that memories are important?

### Boundary breaker 15

# Family relationships

Sometimes boundaries that separate parents or guardians from youth can be bridged through honest sharing. Asking youth and adults to share their feelings with each other is risking hurt as well as hope. After utilizing many of the boundary breakers in this resource book, you may have parents, guardians, and participants who have learned many things about each other.

Discuss these questions together:

◆ What is the most significant thing you have learned about your teenager/parent from this exercise?
◆ Describe the questions and answers that were the hardest for you to share. Why were they difficult?
◆ Would you like to continue sharing in discussions about important feelings together? Why or why not?

### Boundary breaker 16

# Living in faith

As baptized Christians we are called to live in a community of faith. Sometimes we feel that faith is something to be earned, not something that is a gift. The Spirit imparts faith. It is God's work, not ours. God enables our faith to be nurtured as we journey together. This is the purpose of confirmation—to affirm the faith journey begun in the waters of our baptisms.

Remember your baptism and talk about these questions:

◆ If you can remember, describe your baptism. If you were baptized as an infant, have your parent or guardian describe it for you.
◆ How can a person's faith grow stronger?
◆ Who are some people with whom you can share your faith? How can you broaden that circle?

### Boundary breaker 17

# Friends

Being part of a social group gives a young person a feeling of belonging and safety. Having friends to talk to can ease difficult times. When friends betray a youth it can be devastating. Friends are also important to adults. They provide support, affirmation, and are often called upon to help in time of need. It is positive for children and adults to affirm and acknowledge the importance of friends.

Talk about these questions together:

◆ What qualities do you value in those whom you call your friends?
◆ What do you think is the ideal number of close friends? Why do you feel this way?
◆ How do you make up with a friend when she or he has wronged you?

## Boundary breaker 18

# What Jesus means to me

Young adolescents and adults can have a different view of Jesus. To one, Jesus may be like a friend, to another, Jesus is thought of as Savior. Jesus the Christ is revealed to us in the Bible. Jesus also comes to us in the Sacraments of Baptism and the Lord's Supper. These means of grace reveal God's gracious love. During confirmation, we explore the meaning of God in our lives. Parents and sponsors can also learn about God's love in new and fresh ways.

Explore together ways that you experience God's love by talking about these questions:

- The Gospel of John says, "For God so loved the world that he gave his only Son, so that everyone who believes in him may not perish but may have eternal life" (John 3:16). What does this passage say to you about Jesus?
- God comes to us in our reading of the Bible and in our participation in the sacraments. How do people feel that God is near? Are there ways that we might feel closer to God?
- How has your picture of God changed over the years?

## Boundary breaker 19

# Recognizing injustice

Young people are keenly aware of injustice and unfairness. Their experiences in school can be filled with unfairness. Youth can be overlooked because they are not the "best" in the class. Cheaters or people who beat the system can get higher grades than those who do not cheat. In the adult world, promotions can lead to ill feelings between coworkers. Homelessness, accidents, and diseases can strike without cause, leading to feelings of loneliness and unfairness. These issues can plague each of us and make us doubt the power of God.

Discuss together these questions:

- Name one or more problems facing the world today that make us question whether God exists.
- How do you feel when you hear of tragic events that happen to your friends? How can faith in God help you cope?
- Why is it hard for us to feel as upset when tragic things happen to people who live long distances from us?
- What do you do when your faith in God is challenged or when you doubt God's power?

Parent-to-Parent

# Introduction

Providing hope and support to the parents and guardians of young teenagers can be a great gift of your confirmation program. A community of caring adults can quickly develop while they gather to discuss issues that cause concern to them. Parents and guardians are charged with the emotional, physical, and spiritual care of their teenagers. By emphasizing this important role during the confirmation process, you can encourage a nurturing attitude in parents and guardians. This can encourage teenagers who are in confirmation to grow in their faith, within the context of your church community as well as within their own households.

**LEADING ADULT DISCUSSION GROUPS** Send a personal letter pointing out that these parent-to-parent conversations are designed to provide support as they provide affirmation to their students in confirmation. The letter should be invitational, stating the goals and stressing the informality of the sessions. Be sure to provide them with the number of a leader to contact with any questions.

The discussion room should be carefully prepared. The room should be informal, with areas for small group discussion. Use soft furniture if available, and sit in circles or clusters of chairs. Establish a reception area to welcome people as they arrive. Provide name tags and make introductions if people do not know each other.

Setting ground rules for participation should be discussed. Open-ended questions are used in this format because they cannot be answered with simple "yes" or "no" responses. Provide adults with the opportunity to scan their own thoughts, phrase and rephrase, think of stories, and broaden their understanding of faith and life issues. Ask the adult participants to help lay out ground rules such as:

- There are no "right" or "wrong" ideas, only lots of good thoughts.
- We are going to pledge to each other that we will listen carefully, and ask questions when we are not sure whether we have truly heard what the person meant to say.
- We are going to watch ourselves so the conversation is not dominated by the same people.
- We are going to allow people to pass during some questions; not everyone needs to answer every question.
- We are going to keep answers and responses confidential, not sharing another person's ideas with people outside the room.
- We are going to seek to grow in how we understand many of the issues being discussed.

**HOW TO CONDUCT A SESSION** First you will provide the group with a topic and background information. This is provided in "Background." You can read that section out loud or paraphrase it with your own words.

Second, you will provide suggested "Conversations"—questions that help them explore an issue. Feel free to add input or explanation along the way. Not all questions need be asked at once. Use small groups to report back to the whole group if you wish. Parents will probably want to spend the majority of time talking and sharing in small groups rather than listening to what everybody says about each question.

Third, wrap up the conversations through the suggested "Response" activity. Each topic can take up to 20 minutes. To use even a few of the topics will require multiple sessions of parent-to-parent conversations.

Watch carefully for times when the group seems to have completed the topic quickly so you can move on with more discussion themes. And watch, too, for those times when the conversation takes an unexpected turn. These can be great moments for personal sharing and important learning on the part of the adults.

The following topics provide opportunities for parents, guardians, and other adults to discuss the young people they care about. Feel free to think of your own topics or questions after trying some of these. Often there may be specific concerns that are unique to your church setting. Finding and exploring those concerns can keep these exercises relevant.

Relationships

# Getting acquainted

**BACKGROUND** How do people get to know each other in a hurry? They tell stories about themselves. They share laughter and positive feedback. They express feelings of enjoyment to each other.

Sometimes the relationship we have with a teenage son or daughter needs the same interaction. We often assume that we should not, that living under the same roof means we have an intimate relationship. In reality, relationships have to be worked out *together*. It would be wise to share stories with each other—to share feelings, anecdotes, funny memories, and events in our lives with those we love the most.

This conversation will help us get acquainted through the sharing of stories and events in our lives. Take a little extra time with this conversation, so that friendships can be established.

## CONVERSATIONS

- Share an experience from your childhood that stands out in your mind.
- Share a positive experience from your teenage years.
- Share a somewhat embarrassing experience from your teenage years.
- Describe your current situation—your family, work, hobbies, friends, and so on.
- Give an example of something you enjoy doing with your teenage son or daughter.
- Share how you are feeling about participating in these sessions.
- What do you hope your son or daughter might get out of the confirmation experience?
- What hopes do you have for yourself in this process?
- Be honest. Do you think your teenager enjoys confirmation? What is enjoyable? What frustrations does your teenager have about confirmation? Describe the degree of importance your son or daughter places on confirmation.
- What do you enjoy the most about having an adolescent in your family? The least?
- What role do you think the church should play in the life of a teenager?

**RESPONSE** Think back on the conversation you just had. Pair up and repeat to each other something you remember that the other said. Ask the group as a whole what might help them to be better listeners. Encourage things like using good eye contact, rephrasing for people what they have just said to indicate you have heard and understood, and helping people seek the right phrases and feelings to help describe their thoughts.

Relationships

# Enjoying our teens

**BACKGROUND** Many people are eager for their children to grow up and become more like adults. Some parents look forward to more engaging conversation with youth. Some enjoy it when a youth can help with household tasks or assist with projects like car maintenance or running errands. Some are proud of their child's good looks and easygoing lifestyle.

Developing positive relationships with youth is a gift worth developing. Often our youth feel as if parents do not enjoy them. Parents are often seen as people who are out of touch and lack a basic understanding of how to treat them. The disciplinarian role of parents can cause youth to feel powerless in the events of their own lives.

It is inevitable that there will be times of conflict between youth and their parents. At the very time parents feel that they need to control more things, their children begin the process of becoming independent.

**CONVERSATIONS** Use these questions to help you reflect upon and encourage positive qualities of your youth and ways to build strong relationships with them.

◆ Think back on your teenage years. What were you good at? What gave you positive feelings?
◆ What are some positive qualities that you admire in your child?
◆ Name three things your daughter or son is good at doing. How have you encouraged these positive attributes? How could you encourage them in ways that translate positively with your child?
◆ If you could spend more time with your daughter or son, what would you want to do together?
◆ Name something your child likes to do (that is harmless) but that you dislike doing. How might you share in that experience?
◆ Share one way you can support a hobby or interest of your son or daughter.
◆ In what ways are youth being pushed to grow up too quickly? How can you help your youth adjust to these demands or to feel good when not meeting them?

**RESPONSE** Make a pledge to spend time during the coming week in an activity that encourages your daughter or son to develop positive qualities. While participating in this activity, think about how it helps you to grow closer in your relationship with your youth.

### Relationships

# Hobbies and interests

**BACKGROUND** Youth often understand themselves in terms of what they can do. This understanding of self appears to be part of the journey through adolescence. We hope they will begin to value themselves not solely in terms of comparison to others on the basis of their talents, but in terms of their intrinsic worth as a child of God.

At the same time, hobbies and interests of youth can provide wonderful opportunities for adults and their youth to build relationships together. Sharing in activities, whether sewing, fishing, walking, skating, or visiting relatives, can build a bond of friendship and admiration.

Parents and guardians can push too hard when it comes to developing interests. The caricature of the sports coach screaming at a young boy or girl is all too painful. Sometimes parents are eager to provide every opportunity to a young person who shows promise in music, sports, or fine arts. In other homes, providing such opportunities is impossible; parents feel guilty that they have not been good providers. Youth appreciate support, affirmation, and respect for their accomplishments.

**CONVERSATIONS** Use these conversation starters to help in the discovery and the encouragement of interests and abilities of adolescents:

◆ Describe any skills or abilities you have noticed in your youth.
◆ Can you think of other attributes of your youth you appreciate such as humor, positive outlook, leadership among friends, patience, and so forth?
◆ Give suggestions to each other about ways to share in the interests of daughters and sons.
◆ Can you think of something you encouraged your youth to try, but he or she was afraid? How did you encourage him or her? If you wish, share about this experience.
◆ How do you feel when you see a talent or ability in your youth that she or he does not want to use? How might you encourage her or him to use it?
◆ Describe some abilities or talents you had that you never used. Why do you still remember them?
◆ What kinds of hopes do you have for your children?

**RESPONSE** Look for opportunities to link youth with adults. For example, some adults may wish their youth had more opportunities to travel or to see cultural events. Perhaps your church could arrange for summer trips or for a visit to a museum or arts center along with adults who share those interests.

### Relationships

# Music

**BACKGROUND** Youth and their music are inseparable. The hard rhythms of rock are as various as the young people who listen to the music. The background noise of music is a constant at any youth event; it is background for homework, chores, walks, bus rides, or vacation drives. The study of the music that teens love helps us better understand teen culture. The words of songs emphasize themes of which youth are keenly aware: love, broken friendships, uncertain identity, dating, wishing for relationships that do not exist but might!

Going to a youth dance is a sensory experience that blends sight, sound, touch, and smell. Bright lights, crowded dance floors, movement—all create the illusion of total involvement in a community experience. Adults find the enthrallment expressed by some teens toward these experiences to be almost frightening; the power of the moment seems to sweep teens away. Yet adults would be wise to remember their own identification with the artists of rock 'n' roll in their younger years.

Many adults are unaware of the music their teens are hearing. They are unaware of the styles of the groups, the words of their songs, or other characteristics of the music being heard. Music communicates numerous messages. In recent years, groups have been accused of promoting songs with offensive messages that advocate violence and disrespect for the law.

**CONVERSATIONS** Use these questions to help think through how well you know and understand your teenagers and their musical preferences, and how you can interact within this culture.

- Who were your favorite musical groups when you were a young teen?
- If you have ever attended a major rock concert, share your experiences with the group.
- Name one or more of the favorite musical groups of your son or daughter. Can you name any of their songs? Can you recite any of the words?
- Describe as many types of rock as you know about. (For example, light rock, acid rock, punk rock, rap, alternative, and so on.) What are their characteristics?
- How do you determine whether a musical group is offensive to our society?
- Do you feel comfortable letting your youth attend a rock concert? Why or why not?
- How has music changed from the day you were a teenager to today? How did it change from your parent's day to when you were a teenager?
- What are the positive aspects of the music culture of youth?
- List the values that are important to parents and guardians on a chalkboard or chart paper.
- How can we shape the values of youth when they live in a culture filled with violent images?
- Is it important to limit or censor music or television that appears to advocate violence?

**RESPONSE** It may be important, depending upon the conversations that occur here, to suggest that there are times when it is important to agree to disagree. This is appropriate to remember in all relationships, including with your teens. It is also okay to ask questions that challenge others to think beyond their present viewpoints. Always look for opportunities to communicate openly and nonjudgmentally. Continue to find ways to build bridges rather than walls as you communicate with your youth.

Relationships

# TV images

**BACKGROUND** The visual images found on a screen, on a video, or on television have changed the ways in which youth mature. Television is a common feature of nearly all homes in North America. A videocassette recorder may be the one piece of technology common to most youth, regardless of ethnic or economic background.

Sociologists have noted that youth live at multiple levels of consciousness. It is not uncommon to study math, watch television, talk on the phone, and listen to a favorite musical group all at the same time. In some cases, this may encourage a sense of separateness from society. It encourages a short attention span and the inability to see broad solutions to big problems. Youth live in a world of images. The power of up-to-the-minute news broadcasts, vivid details of violence, and sensational television reporting made to look like newscasts all provide images—images that can shape personalities, images that can shape values.

**CONVERSATIONS** Use these questions to help adults talk about fears they may have about the nature and the power of media images on youth.

◆ How has television changed during the past decade?

◆ How do your favorite shows differ from your son's or daughter's favorite shows?

◆ Describe ways in which you believe television or film affects the behavior of youth.

◆ What do "special effects" mean to you? When watching television or a film, which has more power to affect the feelings of your youth—the sounds they hear or the scenes they see? Why?

◆ Tell about a person who did something that you believe can be traced to something he or she saw on television. What makes you sure it happened because of what was seen?

◆ What kinds of responsibilities do parents or guardians have when it comes to determining what can be viewed?

◆ Do you believe you can trust the television or film industry to monitor themselves? Why or why not?

◆ Describe the kinds of youth-oriented films that turn you off. What types have you thought were good?

◆ Describe some of the positive ways in which television and film have affected your children.

◆ How can we encourage the positive use of television and film?

**RESPONSE** Organize a night at the movies for confirmation students and their parents. Have each group pick a video they enjoyed during their teenage years. Watch a portion of each video and talk about why it was chosen, its impact on those who watch, the differences between language and quality (if any), and what makes for a good video. Discuss ideas about a rationale that people might use to support good taste in the film and television industry.

## Physical changes

# Physical growth

**BACKGROUND** During confirmation years, teens experience amazing growth in many ways. To many teens, these changes are exciting; to others, they are frightening. Height and weight changes occur. Muscles develop. Hair appears in new places. A teen's self-image is directly related to her or his physical appearance. One of the major roles of parenting during these years is that of encouraging teens in the areas of self-esteem and confidence during this time of growth and change.

**CONVERSATIONS** Use these ideas to help explore this topic:

- ◆ Share a memory from your adolescent years.
- ◆ Tell about a situation where you remember feeling uncomfortable as a youth.
- ◆ What did you look like when you were the age of your son or daughter? Describe your hairstyle and the clothes you wore.
- ◆ Do you know of a physical characteristic that causes your son or daughter concern?
- ◆ Share ways that you are able to help your son or daughter feel positive about the way he or she looks.
- ◆ What role does clothing play in the way a young person feels?

**RESPONSE** What analogy could you use to describe adolescence? *(An earthquake, an explosion, a metamorphosis.)* The analogies no doubt illustrate a time of great change. When you were a youth, what words did you need to hear from your parent(s)? Did you hear them? Would those same words help your daughter or son now? How can we support our teens in this time of great physical change?

## Physical changes

# Sexuality

**BACKGROUND** Discussing sexuality has become more public in recent years. This is, in part, due to more cultural awareness of the transmission of sexual disease and the public treatment of homosexuality, AIDS, and sexual lifestyle. This does not necessarily mean that parents will find it any easier to discuss sexuality with their children. But sexuality is a common health topic in schools and churches. It should also be discussed openly in homes.

Youth experience profound feelings about their sexuality. As they notice physical changes in their bodies they become more aware of the potency of sexual feelings. Stereotypical behavior may be encouraged by groups of boys or girls. Sexual jokes may perpetuate attitudes that need changing. Pornographic materials are common and can be found in most communities. Images of ideal male and female bodies can be taken from newspapers, magazines, or television. All of these images can create confusing messages about human sexuality.

As parents, guardians, and adults who care about youth, we need to be forthright in our abilities to discuss sexuality. It is, in our society, an issue of life or death. Many adolescent suicides are thought to be attributed to struggles with sexual identity. Sexually active young people can experience grave circumstances (sexually transmitted diseases, pregnancy) before they are mature enough to handle them. If we care about youth, we will attempt to learn the facts, reflect upon our values, and discuss these issues openly with our youth.

**CONVERSATIONS** Use the following questions to help adults in articulating their feelings about the topic of sexuality as it relates to their children, within a context of support and affirmation.

◆ In what ways has public awareness and discussion of human sexuality changed in the last decade?

◆ Think back to when you learned about human sexuality. Compare that to how you believe your teenage son or daughter learned. How is it the same? Different?

◆ Why does our society make such a big deal about sex?

◆ What is the relationship between sexuality and love? Do you believe love is necessary in order to engage in sexual activity? Do these beliefs change depending upon the age of participants?

◆ How do you feel about violent crimes involving rape or sexual abuse? What should be done to perpetrators? For victims?

◆ How do you believe you would respond if a son or daughter told you he or she were gay?

◆ How do you think your youth feels about sexually active friends?

◆ How might the church help parents and youth to shape their values and beliefs about human sexuality?

**RESPONSE** Church members have a difficult time reaching consensus on issues regarding human sexuality. Choose a topic (homosexuality, teen pregnancy, AIDS prevention) and ask the adult participants to come up with a way in which the topic could be addressed in a nonthreatening, nonjudgmental manner in your church. What could be the discussion format? Who might be a resource leader? What kinds of materials could be distributed? How could support groups be developed? Use this exercise to determine whether the group participants are able to agree to be agreeable when discussing difficult issues in the church.

### Emotions

# Building self-esteem

**BACKGROUND** In this section we explore issues such as managing feelings, building self-esteem, friendships, and dating. Use these conversations to help parents discuss issues that can require support and understanding from others.

There is no more important goal in the adolescent years than building a positive sense of self. Positive self-esteem will carry a young person through times of emotional distance or outright failure. Self-esteem enables young people to play an effective role in society; it creates a social acumen necessary to life.

Building positive self-esteem is a spiritual matter as well. It is a mission worthy of the church's time. Self-esteem begins in and through the important relationships in our lives. Victims of tragic home lives can still develop positive self-esteem, encouraged by caring relationships with teachers, neighbors, friends, and church workers.

Positive self-esteem can be encouraged when we affirm unique qualities and help a person to feel good about herself or himself. Self-esteem is nurtured when a person is included and valued by a group. One does not have to be the leader or the most intelligent person in class to develop a positive concept of self. A healthy self-esteem is critical in order to lead a healthy and positive life.

**CONVERSATIONS** Use these questions to help explore the topic of self-esteem as it connects to the relationship between you and your teen.

◆ What was the hardest thing for you to accept about yourself as a youth?

◆ Share an experience when you felt you made a valuable contribution as a young person.

◆ On a scale of 1 to 10, 10 being very positive, rate the level of self-esteem you believe your youth has and explain why.

◆ What have you done to encourage positive self-esteem in your teen?

◆ What have you done for other youth to help improve their self-esteem?

◆ Can you think of suggestions that might help more adults encourage positive self-esteem in young people?

◆ What kind of atmosphere do youth need in which to develop positive self-esteem?
◆ Who are the key adult figures in your youth's life?

**RESPONSE** Brainstorm a list of self-esteem-building suggestions, such as bringing in a motivational speaker, taking a field trip to a ropes challenge course or a location where other trust-building exercises are done, or developing a mentoring program (see the "Mentoring" section of *Community-Building Activities and Games*) between adults and youth. Ask for volunteers to assist in turning some of these suggestions into reality.

### Emotions

# Expressing feelings

**BACKGROUND** Mood swings during teenage years are very common. One moment there is anger and tears due to feelings of being excluded by friends; the next moment there is joy and exuberance because of a phone call from another friend. Emotional reactions to the simplest things can seem powerful.

Feelings are powerful. They carry enormous impact for adolescents. Emotional outbursts are common. Anger and frustration or happiness and optimism can be expressed dramatically and at close intervals. It is helpful for parents and guardians to understand the need for youth to express their feelings in safe environments.

**CONVERSATIONS** Use these questions with adults to encourage the sharing of ways to express feelings that will be helpful in accomplishing effective communication with their youth.
◆ When and where was the last time you exploded with anger or frustration? How did you feel? Was this method of communication effective?
◆ What is your usual reaction when your teenager yells at you? Share ideas about how you might respond constructively at these times.
◆ List skills you have observed in people who are effective listeners.
◆ What are some good listening skills? Rate your own ability to listen on a scale of 1 to 10 (10 being very good).
◆ How can destructive emotions be diffused? Should they be diffused?

**RESPONSE** Have a conversation with your son or daughter at a time when both of you are calm and relaxed, about the ways in which emotions are expressed in your home. Be careful not to sound judgmental. Talk openly about the power of emotions and your willingness to be part of his or her emotional life when you are needed. Discuss ways that such a conversation might be accomplished with other adult participants.

## Emotions

# Supporting positive friendships

**BACKGROUND** Many parents and guardians worry about the friends of their children. Adults know the importance of peer groups in creating or changing behavior. To youth, identifying with a group is an essential task. Attempting to be counterculture through dress, hairstyle, and attitude is an affiliation with a group that stands out as different and unique. Finding a group of friends helps define our self-image; it helps youth determine for themselves their own values, beliefs, and directions. This is what makes good friends so important!

Parents and youth can define "good friends" in different ways. To parents, an ideal friend creates a positive impact on their teen; to a youth, a good friend may be one who accepts, listens, shares interests, and is loyal to him or her. Having good grades, staying out of trouble, or representing certain values may not be the qualities of friendship a teenager seeks.

It is hard to be a teenager. We need to find ways to assist adults in encouraging the kind of friendships that encourage positive self-worth.

**CONVERSATIONS** Use these questions to help explore this topic:

- Did you ever have a friend your parents did not like? What was he or she like? How did your parents' opinion make you feel?
- Name a few of your teenager's friends and tell why you like them.
- What kind of background role can you have that might encourage healthy friendships for your son or daughter?
- How can adults help youth understand the meaning of friendship?
- How can parents discourage friendships that are a negative influence on youth?

**RESPONSE** Recall the story of friendship between David and Jonathan in 1 Samuel 18:1-5. This friendship developed after David killed the giant Philistine. Jonathan demonstrated great affection and loyalty toward David. Later he acted as mediator between David and his father, King Saul, protecting David from his father's jealousy. Talk about the friendship described in this story, and compare it to our understanding of friendship today.

## Emotions

# Dating

**BACKGROUND** Many parents and guardians are eager to see their youth participate in dating rituals. These special friendships are welcomed as a mark of maturity by some parents. Imagining the closeness of such relationships can be nerve-racking and frightening for others.

There are many different types of dating rituals. Patterns can differ depending upon the geographic location, ethnic background, age, and friendship circles. It is safe to assume that youth are becoming sexually active at younger ages, and the rise of sexually transmitted diseases makes sexual activity more risky than it has ever been.

Dating does not always lead to sexual activity. Some dating patterns involve large group activities like going to movies, parties, and activities together. Sometimes making commitments to one person early in the teenage years can slow the development of a positive self-image because the two people may be treated as a couple.

**CONVERSATIONS** Use these questions to explore issues of dating. Human sexuality is touched on in this topic but also has appeared in "Physical Changes," an earlier section.

◆ Recall the people in your life whom you have dated. How did you feel during your first few dates?

◆ How do you think dating has changed today from when you were a teenager?

◆ What scares you the most about seeing your son or daughter date?

◆ Do you think dating would help develop positive self-esteem or hinder it in your youth?

◆ What kinds of rules would you lay down if your youth wanted to date on a regular basis?

◆ Describe what you know about homecoming or prom dates. What have you heard that causes you alarm? What do you think sounds fun and exciting?

◆ When considering youth dating, answer the following:

—At what age would you allow dating to begin?

—If asked, would you reserve a motel room for your son or daughter for prom night?

—What are reasonable hours to be home?

—What do you need to know about the person your youth is dating?

—If asked, what kind of suggestions would you give to your son or daughter about how to have a great date?

**RESPONSE** One of the primary issues surrounding the dating years is trust. Dating often means being alone with another person for periods of time, driving cars or taking public transportation, long phone calls, and spending money. One way that relationships of trust can be encouraged is by making a covenant with your teenager that states *mutually agreed upon* expectations. A covenant agreement could include: picking up your teenager at anytime, any place, without question, if he or she runs into a situation he or she cannot handle; a statement about check-in practices when plans must change. Talk with the adult participants about how this idea might be approached with teenagers in the most positive way.

### Spirituality

# Creating vision

**BACKGROUND** Vision of any kind is important in our journey to adulthood. In the Christian church, we want to provide opportunities to explore what it is that we believe. Use these conversations to help adults explore *their* role in the nurturing of a positive spiritual vision for their youth.

Youth require vision in order to act successfully. Without vision, actions become mechanical. Without vision, schoolwork can seem mundane and repetitive. Without vision, it is difficult to feel motivated. Without hopes and dreams, vision is limited.

Helping youth to develop and capture their own vision is an important role of parenting. Some youth are too idealistic, but the dreams they hold can be adapted to become attainable. Others need encouragement to expand their vision to include hopes and dreams that move them beyond their present realities. It is in finding this balance that youth are able to embark on positive personal growth. Those in parenting roles can help youth in this process by talking positively about the future with them. These conversations can center on the hopes and dreams that are central to the visions your teenager holds.

**CONVERSATIONS** The following may be helpful in your conversation:

◆ Think of a dream you had as a teenager. How did that dream help you, or how didn't it help you, in making decisions?

◆ Who are some of the people you admired the most as a teen? How did their ideals help you shape your life vision at that point in your life?

◆ What are some of the dreams of your daughter or son? How might you learn more about them?

◆ Who are some of the people your teenager admires?

◆ What qualities do you have that you believe your teenager admires?
◆ How do you help youth think about the future?
◆ Describe a dream that became reality for you in your youth. How did you feel? What were the steps that caused the dream to become reality?
◆ Does your son or daughter have special dreams? How might you help him or her attain these dreams?
◆ What role can faith play in the creation of vision?

**RESPONSE** Encourage parents and guardians to talk about the future with their youth during the coming week. Encourage them to share their dreams and visions first, then ask their youth to share. Sometimes a far-reaching vision can be broken down into attainable steps. Encourage taking one step at a time to build toward a vision.

### Spirituality

# Faith life

**BACKGROUND** Many parents struggle with keeping their children involved in the life of the church. As a Christian community, the church may seem dull and boring to young people. To some it comes across as trivial, to others, out of touch. The formality of some worship settings bothers some youth. Yet studies have shown that youth are highly religious. Many have regular prayer practices and believe in God. A majority would claim that what they believe shapes their actions and behavior.

**CONVERSATIONS** Use these questions to explore the importance of Christian faith in the lives of youth and adults:
◆ Why is it so hard to keep youth involved in the life of the church? How does Christian faith shape life?
◆ Share a memory from your early faith experiences.
◆ On a scale from 1 to 10, 10 being very comfortable, how comfortable are you talking about your faith in Jesus Christ with your teenagers?
◆ Describe how you have tried to create a Christian environment in your home.
◆ Describe the last time you had a conversation about your beliefs with your daughter or son.
◆ How important do you feel religion is to your daughter or son?
◆ What kind of concerns about faith issues do you think are important to young people? Do they have a chance to explore those concerns in confirmation?
◆ In what ways are parents responsible for nurturing the faith of their teenagers? In what way is the church responsible? How successful would you rate yourself and your church in this endeavor?
◆ How important is it to be in regular attendance in Christian worship?
◆ What are your goals for the confirmation program that your child attends?
◆ Name three ways you might be able to talk more about your Christian beliefs with your daughter or son.
◆ How might your pastor or church workers be more helpful in assisting young people to explore their Christian faith?

**RESPONSE** The role adults play in the faith lives of youth cannot be underestimated. Actions speak louder than words. Participation in faith activities by parents and guardians can Inspire participation by youth. Likewise, negative comments about worship, the church staff, and the messages that are proclaimed are absorbed by teenagers and revealed in their attitudes about church. List a series of ways in which parents and guardians can promote a positive image of church, and encourage youth in a life of faith.

## Spirituality

# Youth and God's Word

**BACKGROUND** Nurturing Christian growth in an adolescent is an opportunity parents and guardians often overlook. Many adults feel that young people are not interested in Christian growth. Because of this assumption, they do not often attempt to encourage a young person to explore his or her development as a creature of faith. This responsibility is often left to the church.

God's Word needs to be at the center of adolescent life. In order for young Christians to identify with the Christian faith, they need to hear and respond to the biblical story. If we believe in the power of the Holy Spirit to call, gather, and enlighten, we should not keep the basic symbols of our faith from our adolescents. They view their own lives as part of God's plan. They need and remember resources that help them along their journeys. They struggle with what it means to be created in God's image.

We believe that Word and Sacrament are the chief means through which God's grace is brought to bear on the life of a believer. Use these questions to consider ways of encouraging the use of God's Word among youth. Explore ways in which adults model behavior that lifts up the importance of the Bible.

**CONVERSATIONS**

◆ Share a Bible passage that is meaningful to you. How has it impacted your life?
◆ Talk about a time when you found a Bible passage to have helped you during a personal crisis or faith struggle.
◆ Is Bible reading a regular part of your life? Has it ever been? What kind of reading plan do (or did) you follow?
◆ How might Bible reading be more interesting and exciting to readers?
◆ Why might youth enjoy regular Bible reading?
◆ What are some of the barriers youth have that prevent regular Bible reading? How might you help overcome these barriers?
◆ How might it be possible to encourage Bible reading together with your adolescent?

**RESPONSE** Sometimes Bible reading is problematic because people find some of the texts difficult to understand. Talk about the various versions of the Bible. Encourage them to use versions that are fairly easy to understand (Today's English Version and the New Revised Standard Version). Have resources available to help them in their Bible reading with their sons or daughters. New Venture in Bible Reading: *Bible Ventures 1*, *Bible Ventures 2*, *Bible Ventures 3* (Minneapolis: Augsburg Fortress, 1990, 1992, 1992) offers a Bible reading plan. There is a three-track Bible reading outline in *Study Bible: The New Student Bible NRSV* as well. Other devotional helps are appropriate as well. Emphasize the hearing of the story and the power of the words in revealing the person of Jesus Christ.

Spirituality

# Participation in worship

**BACKGROUND** Confirmation programs rely on Word and Sacrament to help young people identify with the Christian community and participate fully in its mission. This means, of course, attendance and participation in worship. It is difficult to follow through on this emphasis without the support of adults. The confirmation experience involves more than youth. Youth live in relationship with others in their households. It is difficult (but not impossible) for youth to participate in church without their parents. Parents participating in these conversations are probably aware that they have a responsibility to share in the leadership of confirmation. Worshiping together is a significant way of doing this.

What happens in worship? There are three important books for Lutherans: the Bible proclaims the good news of Jesus; *Lutheran Book of Worship* uses biblical texts and liturgy to enable a community of believers to worship; Luther's Small Catechism interprets the chief components of worship. These three books create a healthy framework for Christian faith and life within the worshiping community.

**CONVERSATIONS** The previous parent conversation asked questions about the use of the Bible in confirmation homes. Use this conversation to explore worship life and, in particular, the importance of the Sacraments of Holy Baptism and Holy Communion:

◆ What do you believe happens in worship?
◆ Describe some of your favorite worship festivals. Think of events such as Christmas Eve, Palm Sunday, or another meaningful worship event.
◆ Name as many different parts of the worship service as you can. Do you have a favorite part in the liturgy? Tell about it.
◆ What does Baptism mean to you? Why is it good for a congregation to be part of a Baptism?
◆ What does Holy Communion mean to you? Do you find each communion as meaningful as any other? How have communion practices changed over the years?
◆ How active should we expect a confirmation youth to be in worship? Does our worship service succeed in being meaningful to our youth?
◆ How could our worship service be changed to be more sensitive to youth as valued members of the congregation?

**RESPONSE** Confirmation is called "Affirmation of Baptism." Provide a *Lutheran Book of Worship* for each participant to explore the questions used in the service of the Affirmation of Baptism beginning on page 198. Then turn to page 121 and compare the questions asked of parents or sponsors during a service of Baptism. What differences do they see? What similarities? In these questions, confirmands are affirming the promises which were made on their behalf during Baptism. Considering the promises of baptism and the service of affirmation, church participation should take on a very prominent position. At the same time, church worship leaders need to be sensitive to the needs of youth who will attend services. Evaluate together your church's worship life from this perspective.

## Spirituality

**BACKGROUND** In many cases, parents may remember having to study Luther's catechism during confirmation. They may remember (unkindly!) long periods in which they had to memorize or learn the meaning of the catechism. Memory work in confirmation has often been criticized. There have been many instances, however, where memorized verses, hymns, and the catechism have provided life-sustaining help for people during times of trial. Such was the case with Katherine Koob when she was kept in captivity for many months. She remembered hymns, prayers, and verses, and used them regularly to sustain her.

We ought not to criticize memory work too harshly. After all, most youth can recite endless verses to their favorite rock songs. It is not hard for them to remember word for word hundreds of songs, favorite television ads, and any number of other trivial points. But when it comes to church memory work, there are always complaints not only from youth but from parents and guardians as well.

For more background see *A Contemporary Translation of Luther's Small Catechism* where the introduction tells more about what Luther did and why.

**CONVERSATIONS** Use these questions to explore the use of the catechism (it would be helpful to have copies available to read) during the confirmation years and the feelings parents have about it:

◆ What is Luther's catechism? How would you explain it to someone who hadn't heard of it before?

◆ What does Luther seek to teach about in the catechism?

◆ Did you ever have to memorize portions of the catechism? How did you feel about this task?

◆ What is important for your youth to learn about the catechism? How could they learn about the Ten Commandments, the Apostles' Creed, and the sacraments in the catechism in the best possible way?

◆ Why is it or is it not unrealistic to use memorization techniques to learn the catechism?

◆ Can you think of ways your church could teach the catechism more effectively to youth?

◆ For whom was the catechism written? *(Martin Luther wrote it for parents so they could teach their children!)*

◆ Whose job is it to teach the catechism now? How might parents and guardians enter more fully into this process? (The Creative Confirmation *Family Book* offers a number of ideas.)

**RESPONSE** Distribute the Small Catechism if you have not already done so. Invite adults to explore them. Let them keep the copies and ask them to share a few thoughts about the catechism with their teenagers.

## Spirituality

# Christian service

**BACKGROUND** Service to others is a natural response to the gospel. We love because Christ first loved us. Confirmation programs often include Christian service projects. The *Mission/Service Projects* resource book offers many ideas for encouraging interest and the development of skills in areas of volunteer service. Some adolescents experience volunteer opportunities first during these years.

**CONVERSATIONS** Use these questions to explore how Christian service extends the faith we have into our everyday living:

◆ Think of some ways you have been involved in Christian service. Share an example.
◆ Name some Christian service projects that happen in your congregation. *(Spring and fall cleanup days, acolyting, teaching Sunday school, and so forth.)*
◆ How does your congregation show that it cares for people? *(Hospital visits, counseling, celebrations, and so forth.)* How do members of your congregation connect with this caring? *(Stephen ministry, communing shut-ins, adopting new member families, and so forth.)*
◆ Name some service project opportunities in your community. How can participation in such projects connect with our faith?
◆ How is it difficult to encourage youth to participate in service for others? How might we help them see service as opportunity, and a natural response for us as Christians?
◆ How might we see our vocations as opportunities for Christian service? Give examples of possible ways you can serve others through your vocation.

**RESPONSE** Youth want to serve in significant ways. Talk about a service opportunity in your community that could involve the confirmation participants and other family members. How could you work together to make a real difference?

## Attitudes and behaviors

# Responsibility

**BACKGROUND** We love our youth. At the same time, we often try to change them. This seems paradoxical. We love our youth just as they are, but we also want to encourage them to be responsible and loving. Unfortunately, attempting to change behavior can be frustrating for adults, and degrading for youth. Use the conversation starters in this section to explore some of the ways to deal positively with negative behaviors and attitudes of youth.

Teenagers often frustrate the attempts of their parents or guardians to make them responsible. The definition of *responsibility* is often quite different for adults and for teenagers. An adult might expect a teenager to be motivated, on time, responsible with chores, and responsible enough to communicate everything from personal needs to Friday night's plans. To many teens, however, being responsible is placing the needs of their friends before the needs of their family life. Peer loyalty and care of self are higher priorities for many teens than fulfilling the demands of parents.

Parenting literature abounds with suggestions on teaching responsibility. Among the most common is having clear and defined prescriptions to institute when a youth does not fulfill his or her end of the bargain. For example, coming home late without checking in means no going out next Friday night. Penalties are not punishment. They are simply the logical consequences of certain behaviors. When used effectively, they can help teach responsibility.

**CONVERSATIONS** Use the following questions and exercises to explore the meaning of responsibility and how it can be nurtured in teenagers.
◆ Define responsibility. What does it mean when applied to a teenager? How would your teenager define responsibility at this time?
◆ Discuss some significant negative behaviors you experienced as a youth, such as alcohol abuse, drug use, trouble with the law, and so forth.
◆ Describe a number of ways in which your teenage son or daughter has shown responsibility.
◆ What behaviors of your son or daughter irk you the most? How do you deal with it? How have you helped or hindered these situations by your choice of action?
◆ How would your son or daughter describe the trust that you have for him or her? Would your teenager believe that you believe he or she is responsible? How do you respond when other people make positive comments about your teenager?
◆ Name some areas you are unwilling to allow your teenager to be completely responsible for.
◆ Name some of the areas where you would gladly delegate responsibility to your teenager.

◆ Do you believe your son or daughter is more responsible to others than to you? How does this make you feel?

**RESPONSE** Find information about parenting opportunities or support groups in your area. Share this information with your parents and guardians. Ask how these parent conversations have helped support the process of parenting confirmation youth.

### Attitudes and behaviors

# Deadlines

**BACKGROUND** Helping adolescents meet deadlines and keep commitments can be a great challenge. Watching youth cram at the last minute for a test, not turning in permission slips (or even bringing them home), or missing opportunities because of late applications is frustrating. Part of the problem may be lack of motivation of youth. But they are also generally extremely busy, as well as being preoccupied with people, places, and, in general, the youth culture.

**CONVERSATIONS** Use these questions to explore ways to motivate teenagers to do things on time:
◆ Describe something you missed out on because you failed to meet a deadline.
◆ Pretend your son or daughter comes home and finds this list of things to do. What items on this list would your teenager do first, and why?
Take out the garbage.
Return a phone call to a friend.
Turn on the television.
Do homework.
Turn on a boom box.
Clean their room.
◆ How do you motivate teenagers to do homework? Household or outside chores? Complete forms they need for school activities or projects? Talk to you about something important?
◆ Describe some of the consequences students have when they fail to meet deadlines. Who worries more about these consequences, you or your youth? Who *should* worry about them?
◆ How can those of us in parenting roles effectively encourage responsibility in our teenagers in light of these conversations?

**RESPONSE** Do you believe that your teenager's world is too demanding of her or his time? How might we be supportive of our adolescents in light of the pressures they experience? When is the right time to challenge? How can we do so positively?

## Attitudes and behaviors

# Money

**BACKGROUND** Why do some teenagers always have money and others never have enough? For youth, money is a ticket to endless attractions and entertainment. It is a short-term solution to boredom. Youth and adults can differ dramatically in how they understand the importance of money. Youth often seek instant gratification. Money can be understood by teenagers as a right—something they deserve. How much an item costs doesn't seem to matter to many youth. Some youth have more disposable income than adults. For others, the case is quite the opposite. In any case, learning to be a wise steward of money can be an important step in the journey through these confirmation years.

**CONVERSATIONS** Use these questions to explore the roles money can play in the lives of teenagers and adults:

◆ How do we encourage both generosity and common sense when it comes to money? How can young people be taught the wonder of stewardship of all of life's gifts, money included?

◆ Are your children better or worse off financially than you were when you were a young person? In what ways?

◆ Do you believe your son or daughter has made progress in learning the value of money? In what ways?

◆ If you could change anything about the way your teenager handles money, what would it be?

◆ By your actions, what have you been teaching your son or daughter about:
how to give money?
how to save money?
how to spend money wisely?

◆ What are some benefits of being a generous giver?

◆ When are you old enough to begin a regular plan of giving?

◆ How have you shared information with your son or daughter about home budgeting, managing money, or doing taxes?

**RESPONSE** When students are confirmed they usually receive their own offering envelopes. Talk about ways in which the church might help youth handle their money more effectively.

## Attitudes and behaviors

# Teens at work

**BACKGROUND** Youth today can spend many hours baby-sitting or mowing lawns for neighbors. Older youth may turn an endless number of hamburgers and never see a customer. Youth look forward to getting a job and earning money. It is important to consider the topic of youth jobs for a number of reasons. Youth jobs can encourage responsible behavior if the employer is positively geared toward working with youth.

Sometimes jobs are not helpful in developing responsible activity, social skills, or inspiring reflection about future vocational goals. They can require time away from schoolwork, social activities, church, family, or other positive learning opportunities. Sometimes youth can learn how to cheat on time cards, or get by doing as little as possible in low-paying jobs. Having a job is not always a positive experience for youth.

Youth jobs, combined with extensive extracurricular school activities, make a traditional senior high church youth group difficult to achieve. The church needs to explore new ways to support parents and youth in a complicated culture.

**CONVERSATIONS** Confirmation participants may not have entered the world of part-time jobs as yet, but those possibilities lurk on the not too distant horizon. Explore the topic of youth jobs with these questions:

◆ Talk about the jobs you had when you were an adolescent. How are they the same or different than jobs for youth today?

◆ In your opinion, when are you old enough to have a job? How many hours a day is enough? How many hours a week should young people work? What are the best kind of jobs for youth to have and why? Should youth be required to save a portion of their work earnings? Does earning money lead to more spending?

◆ Are you concerned about the kind of people your son or daughter may someday work with? How would you find out about them?

◆ How can parents and guardians improve work conditions for youth in their communities?

◆ Would you allow your teenager to work on Sunday mornings during traditional church times? Why or why not?

**RESPONSE** Encourage parents and guardians to discuss future career possibilities with their youth. Talk about ways that such a conversation could be introduced so that it inspires hopefulness and communicates caring and support, not pressure and preconceived expectations.

### Attitudes and behaviors

# Discipline

**BACKGROUND** Changing behavior is one task most parents and guardians face sooner or later. We call it "discipline." Discipline is not simply punishment. Discipline has to do with altering behavior. We attempt, through discipline, to prevent certain actions from happening again. It is necessary to help young people understand that life has limits. We need to stay within boundaries so life can be full and rewarding for everybody.

Too often we hear of situations where discipline goes overboard. Domestic violence and abuse can be the result of discipline gone awry. Parenting classes often deal with discipline. Discipline needs to be appropriate for the situation. Minor infractions when met with severe punishments make no sense and give mixed messages to youth.

**CONVERSATIONS** Use these questions to explore the ways that parents and guardians understand discipline as it affects them in daily life with their youth.

◆ Think of a strict disciplinarian and an easy one from your past life experiences. Tell about a memory, and what you thought about the incident. Have your ideas changed since that time?

◆ Do you consider yourself strict or do you easily give in? Share some thoughts about your disciplinarian style.

◆ If there is more than one person parenting teens in your home, what are some of the different roles you have when it comes to discipline?

◆ Describe a situation in which you needed to discipline your son or daughter. What do you think he or she learned from the situation? What did you learn from the outcome of the situation and your action?

◆ Why should your disciplinary actions match the situation? Talk about appropriate methods and their connected situations. (It may be helpful to remember conversations about penalties as being logical consequences for negative actions. See page 27.)

◆ Have you ever modeled behavior that you later reprimanded your teenager for copying? Share an example from your own life or someone you know.

**RESPONSE** List the following actions on a chalkboard: stealing, cheating on a test, making a racial slur against someone, coming home late, swearing at a parent, skipping school. Have the adults list appropriate forms of discipline for each example. Discuss ways in which discipline can be filled with grace. Read and discuss Luke 17:3-4. What do these verses say about discipline and forgiveness?

### Attitudes and behaviors

# Chemical abuse

**BACKGROUND** Major problems and crime arise from alcohol and chemical abuse. Though chemical abuse problems are dealt with through public school programs, television, and media, abuse remains a terrifying problem for parents, youth, and all of society. Experimentation with alcohol and chemicals is something that takes place with alarming regularity at young ages. It will not be uncommon for confirmation students to have already experienced the feelings associated with alcohol consumption or drug abuse. Most likely they will all know where to get either alcohol or drugs, and could probably purchase samples readily. It is a stressful reality that the issue of alcohol and drug abuse is something all teenagers will need to face in order to successfully develop their own positive self-image.

Parents face these problems as well. Their lives may have already been dramatically altered by the effects of drugs and/or alcohol. All will know people who have used and abused. Some of the adults participating in these conversations may themselves be struggling with these issues.

**CONVERSATIONS** Use this conversation to explore and discuss the problem of drug abuse, and resources that are available locally that help adults and youth in addressing the issues associated with alcohol and chemical substances.

- What worries do you have about the prominence of alcohol and drugs in our youth culture?
- How do you believe your community, or the youth in your church, struggle with alcohol and chemical abuse?
- What do you think should be done to people who sell drugs and alcohol to youth?
- Do you know adults or parents who have provided alcohol products for the parties of their youth?
- Discuss whether it is ever permissible for underage youth to consume alcoholic beverages.
- What message do you believe the church should offer young people who must face decisions about alcohol and drug abuse?
- Do you know youth who live in homes where alcohol or drug abuse is a problem? What can you do for them?
- Where would you go to get information about chemical abuse?
- If you suspected your son or daughter of abusing chemicals, what would you do? Where would you go for help?
- How can parents and guardians support each other when people they love abuse chemicals or alcohol?
- What can you say to your teenage youth about these issues?

**RESPONSE** Make a list of questions that need advice and information from an expert. Invite a licensed counselor who works with youth who abuse chemicals to your church for a meeting with this group of adults. Share the list of questions with this person. Ask her or him to provide information about possible causes of alcohol and drug abuse. Invite the person to share resources that will help prevent substance abuse or assist those who are already abusing.

## Attitudes and behaviors

# Trouble with the law

**BACKGROUND** Many parents and guardians have teenagers who get in trouble with the law. Most crimes committed by juveniles are handled by a juvenile court system. In some extreme cases, juveniles can be tried in adult courts. Of course, not all teens get in trouble. But if they do, it can be helpful for parents to know that there are systems in place and people who can help. Although parents can play a vital role, most are unprepared to deal effectively with juvenile crime because they are distraught with emotion and confusion.

Systems for dealing with juvenile crimes vary from place to place. Contact the court system in your locality to learn about the systems in place where you live. Most of the time when teens get into trouble, particularly for minor offenses, they are not removed from their homes. The systems are designed to help teens return home to their family and friends. Trained adults assist teens in changing behavior patterns that are harmful. Most of the time teens who get into trouble with the law get help so that they can return to society. The majority are not repeat offenders as we sometimes assume.

**CONVERSATIONS** Use this conversation to explore questions about juvenile systems and to better understand what is in place where you live.

- ◆ If you have ever been in trouble with the law tell of your experiences and what the system was like. (If no one has, share information from the opening paragraphs of this conversation.)
- ◆ Name the most important thing you can do that could help prevent your daughter or son from getting in trouble with the law.
- ◆ When you know a youth who has been in legal trouble, does this affect how you look at him or her?
- ◆ Do you believe that a person is innocent until proven guilty? Why or why not?
- ◆ Can you think of some ways that you might support a friend whose son or daughter got into legal troubles?
- ◆ How can a church provide support for families who have juveniles who are in trouble with the law?
- ◆ Would you encourage someone who had been in a detention center to go on a youth activity with your church? Would you let your daughter or son room with her or him at a youth gathering or camp event?

**RESPONSE** If there is interest in learning more about this topic, plan a date to invite a juvenile worker from your county offices to meet with your adult participants. This person could provide additional information and answer questions regarding the juvenile system and how it works. Find out about the most common juvenile citations and arrests. Ask for advice about things that parents and guardians can do to prevent their youth from breaking the law in the first place.